AN INTRODUCTION TO THE WONDERFUL WORLD OF ROBOTICS

SCIENCE BOOK FOR KIDS

CHILDREN'S SCIENCE EDUCATION BOOKS

Speedy Publishing LLC

40 E. Main St. #1156

Newark, DE 19711

www.speedypublishing.com

Copyright 2017

n this book, we're going to talk about the amazing world of robotics. So, let's get right to it!

Science fiction stories and movies often show robots as moving machines that look something like humans. However, not all robots look like people.

Some are built to function like a person's arm, some just look like machines, and some even look like animals.

WHAT IS A ROBOT?

Roboticists are scientists who create robots. Not all roboticists agree on the true definition of a robot, but most agree that types of software that perform certain jobs are "bots" instead of robots. Usually, when we think of a robot, we think of a machine that has some type of movement.

ROBOT PROTOTYPE

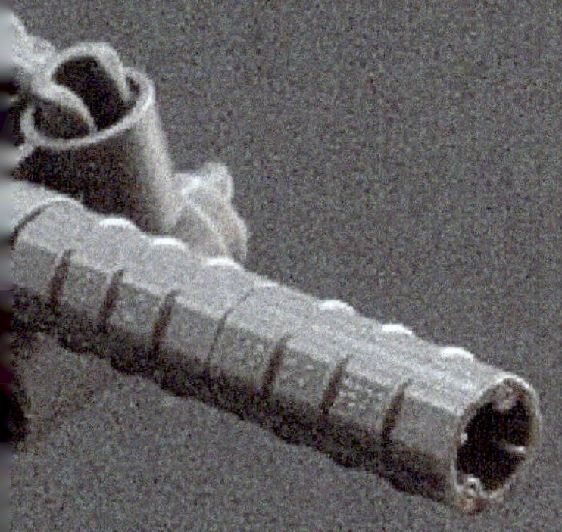

R obots are programmed by people to perform specific tasks. They can do some or all of the following:

- Move from one place to another

- Useamechanicallimbtodosomething, usually a repetitive action

- Sense their surroundings

- ⟲ Manipulate or change their environment in some way

- ⟲ Mimicaspecificbehaviorofahumanorananimal

- ⟲ Show problem-solving and learning abilities

- ⟲ Display a form of intelligence

WHAT FIELDS OF STUDY ARE IMPORTANT TO ROBOTICS?

In order to be a roboticist, you really have to understand a lot about construction, engineering, and computer science. Roboticists are experts in three different scientific fields:

- Mechanical engineering, which deals with the actual mechanical structure of robots

- Electrical engineering, which deals with the electrical systems needed to create the sensing features of robots

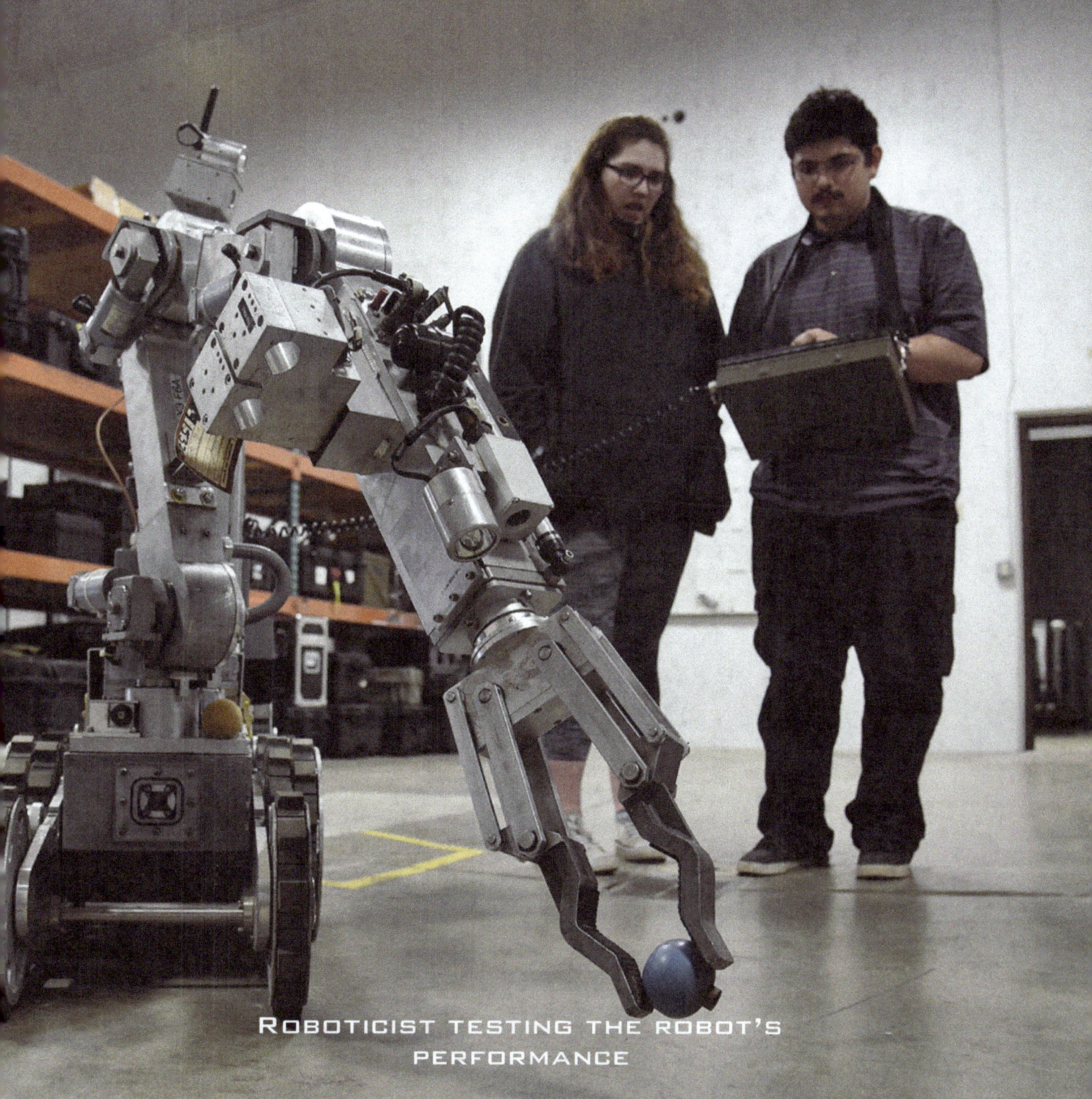

ROBOTICIST TESTING THE ROBOT'S
PERFORMANCE

NASA Tests New Robotic
Refueling Technologies

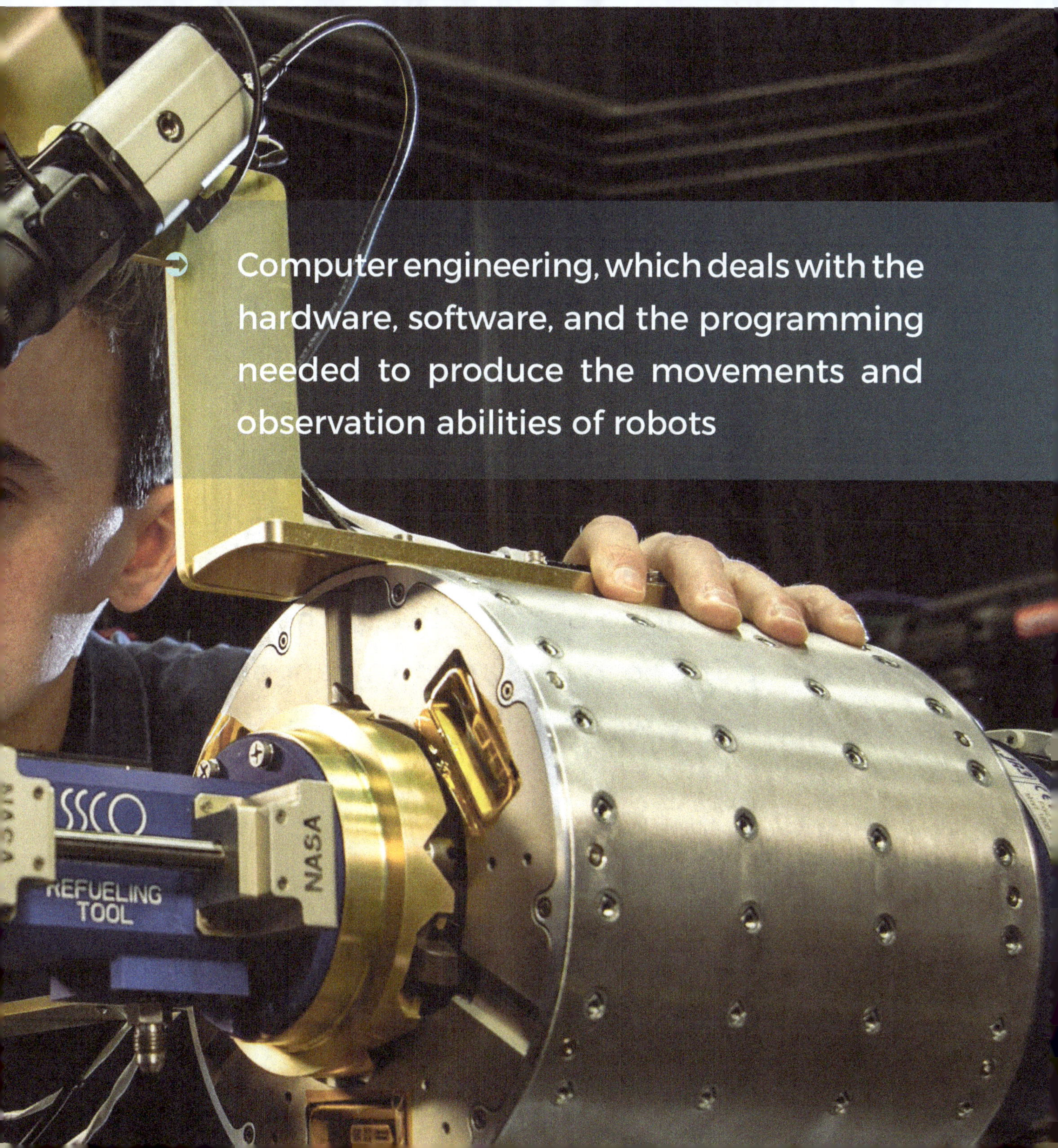
Computer engineering, which deals with the hardware, software, and the programming needed to produce the movements and observation abilities of robots

One of the advantages of having robots in our daily lives is that they can do work that gets really boring or repetitive without getting worn out. They can also perform dangerous jobs so that people won't get hurt.

INDUSTRIAL ROBOT

FOATER-MILLER TALLON ROBOT

For example, they can work with explosive devices or harmful chemicals. They can also work handling dangerous biological cultures. They can travel beyond our solar system to take samples on the surface of Mars or go down to the very depths of the oceans to find new life forms. Some robots are just designed for fun and entertainment too!

The idea of creating an artificial "lifeform" has fascinated mankind for centuries.

270 BC

Ctesibius, who was an engineer in ancient Greece, constructed water clocks that had moving figures.

1818 AD

The author Mary Shelley wrote the novel "Frankenstein." It was about an artificial being that was given life by Dr. Frankenstein.

1921

The word "robot" was introduced in a script for a play called **Rossum's Universal Robots.** The plot was written by Karel Capek, a writer from Czechoslovakia. The storyline was one that would be repeated in different forms for decades afterwards. Man creates a robot. Robot becomes powerful and intelligent. Robot kills his creator.

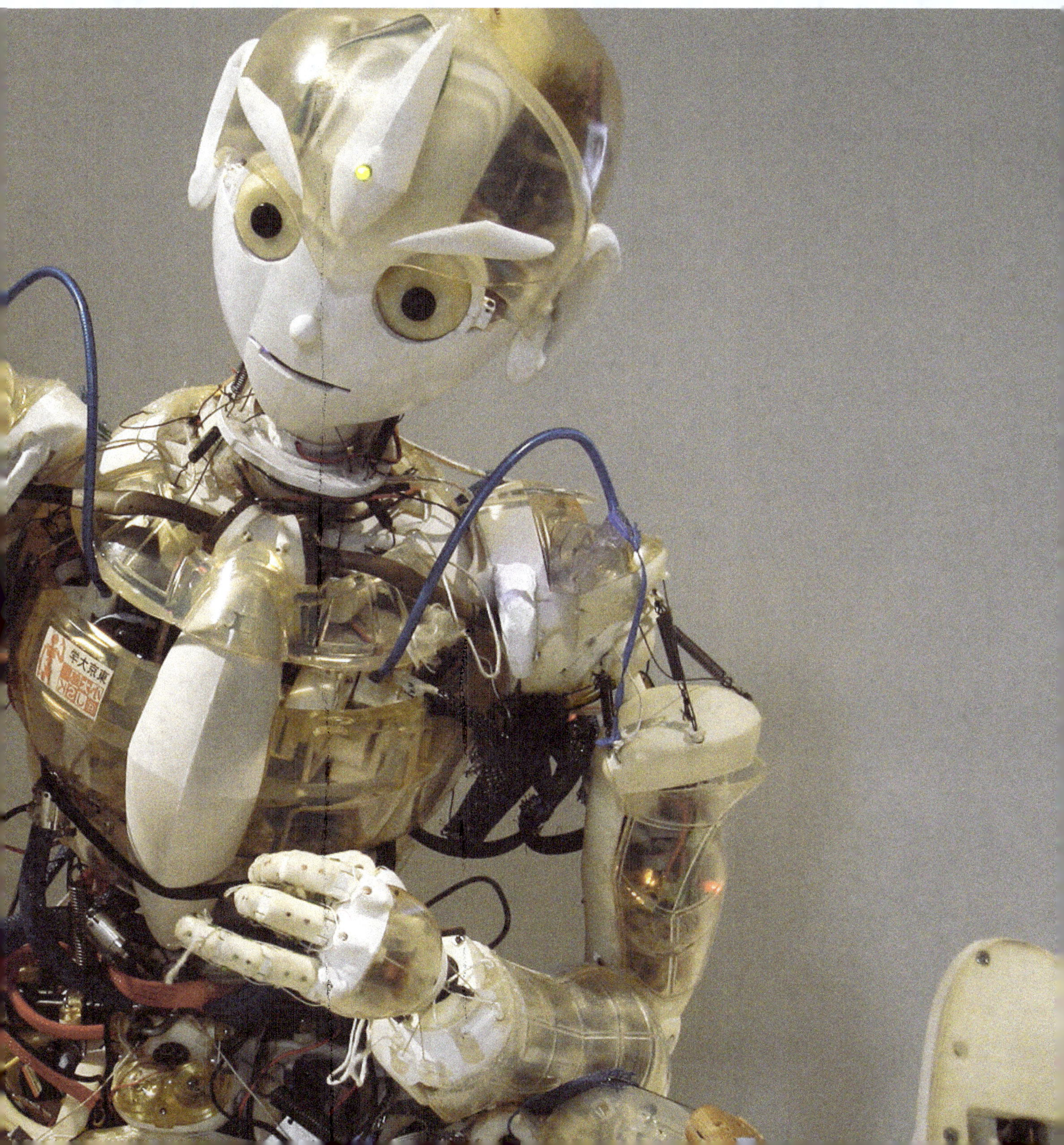

ASIMOV'S THE MOON

1941

The famous science fiction author Isaac Asimov coined the word "robotics" to explain a new science that would be about designing robots and their underlying technology.

1942

Isaac Asimov wrote an interesting story about a space robot, which introduced three "laws of robotics." Robots weren't supposed to harm humans, but must obey humans unless the humans were asking the robots to harm other humans.

1948

The author Norbert Wiener wrote "Cybernetics," which was a study of how animals, humans, and machines store and control information. The book became influential in the study of artificial intelligence.

1956

The world's first company to create robots was formed in New Jersey by founders Devol and Engelberger.

Norbert Wiener

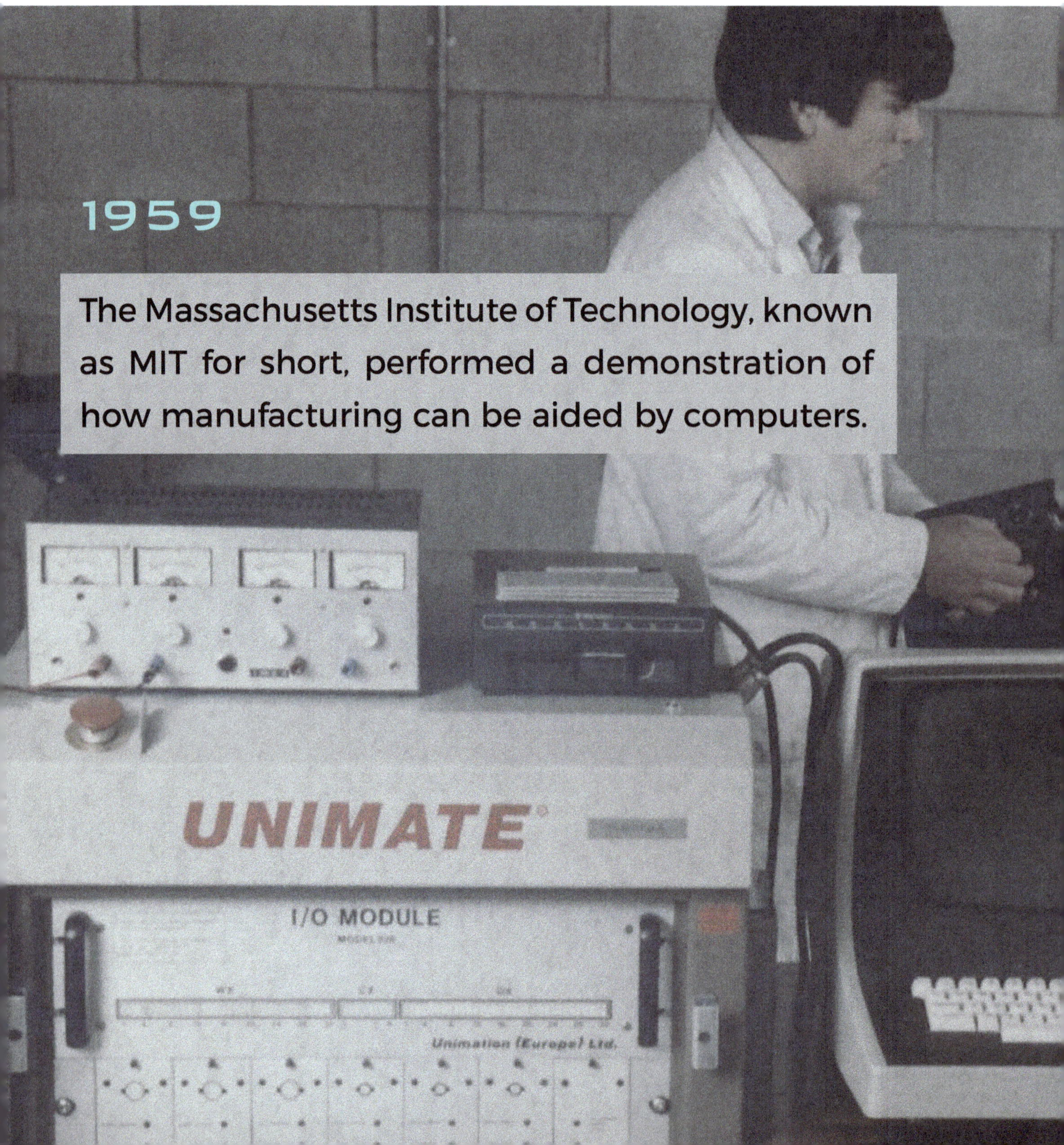

1959

The Massachusetts Institute of Technology, known as MIT for short, performed a demonstration of how manufacturing can be aided by computers.

UNIMATE

I/O MODULE

Unimation (Europe) Ltd.

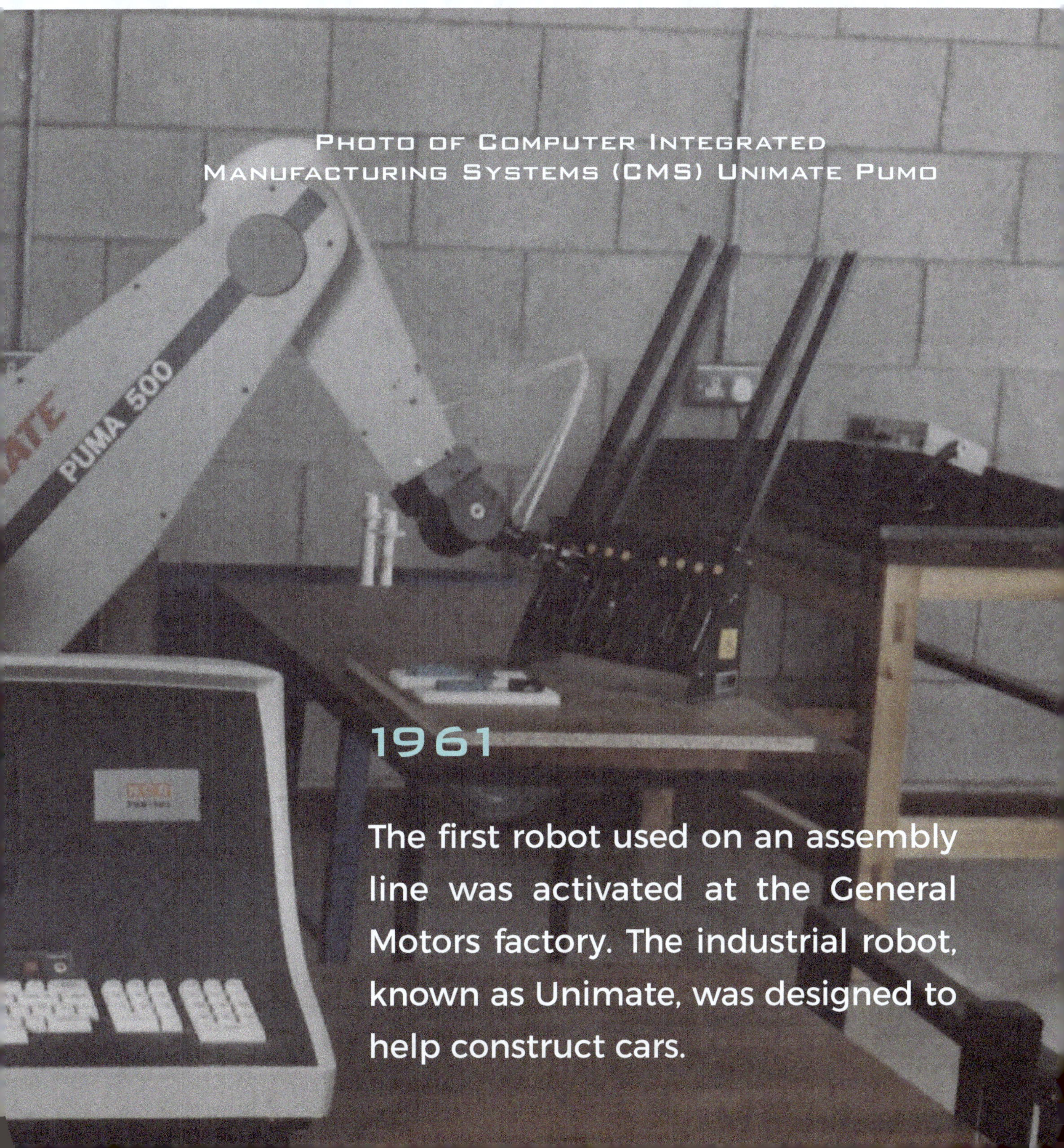

Photo of Computer Integrated Manufacturing Systems (CMS) Unimate Pumo

1961

The first robot used on an assembly line was activated at the General Motors factory. The industrial robot, known as Unimate, was designed to help construct cars.

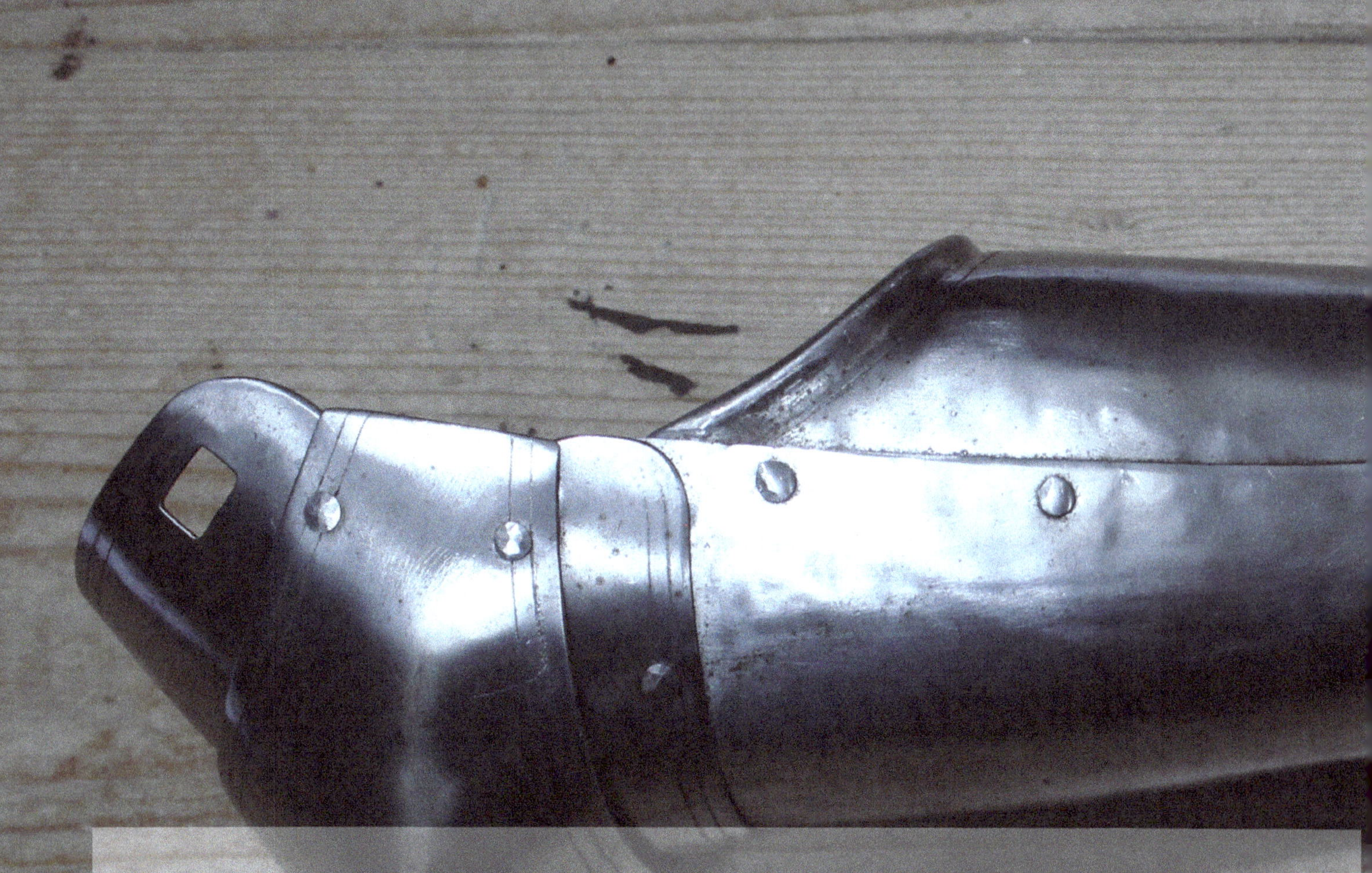

1963

The first robotic limb, called the Rancho Arm after the hospital where it was designed in California, was created for handicapped people. It had six flexible joints so that it could move like a human arm.

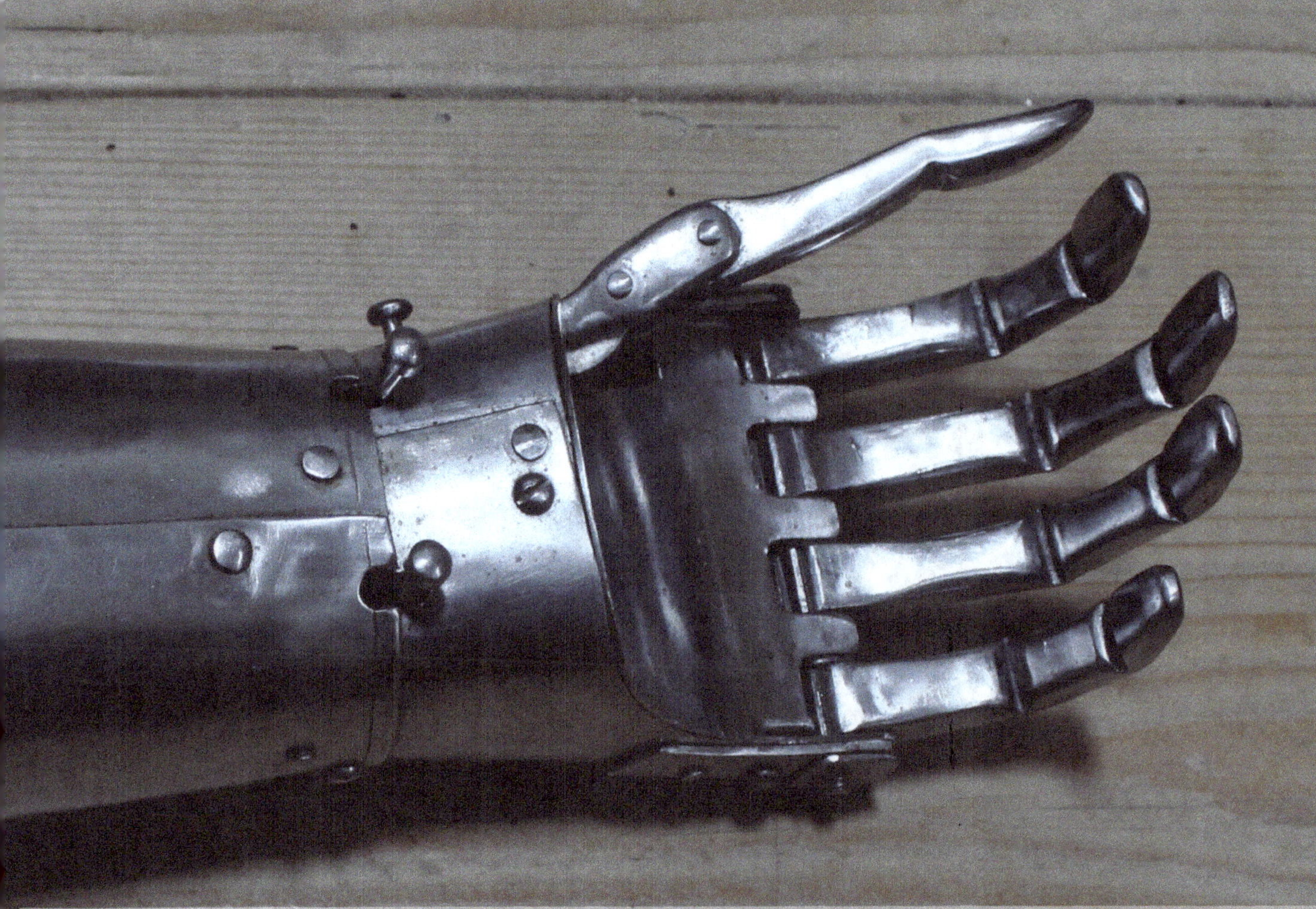

1965

Dendral was an early form of artificial intelligence. It was designed to take information from subject experts to help organic chemists. It was used to identify and form hypotheses about unknown organic molecules. A team at Stanford University created Dendral.

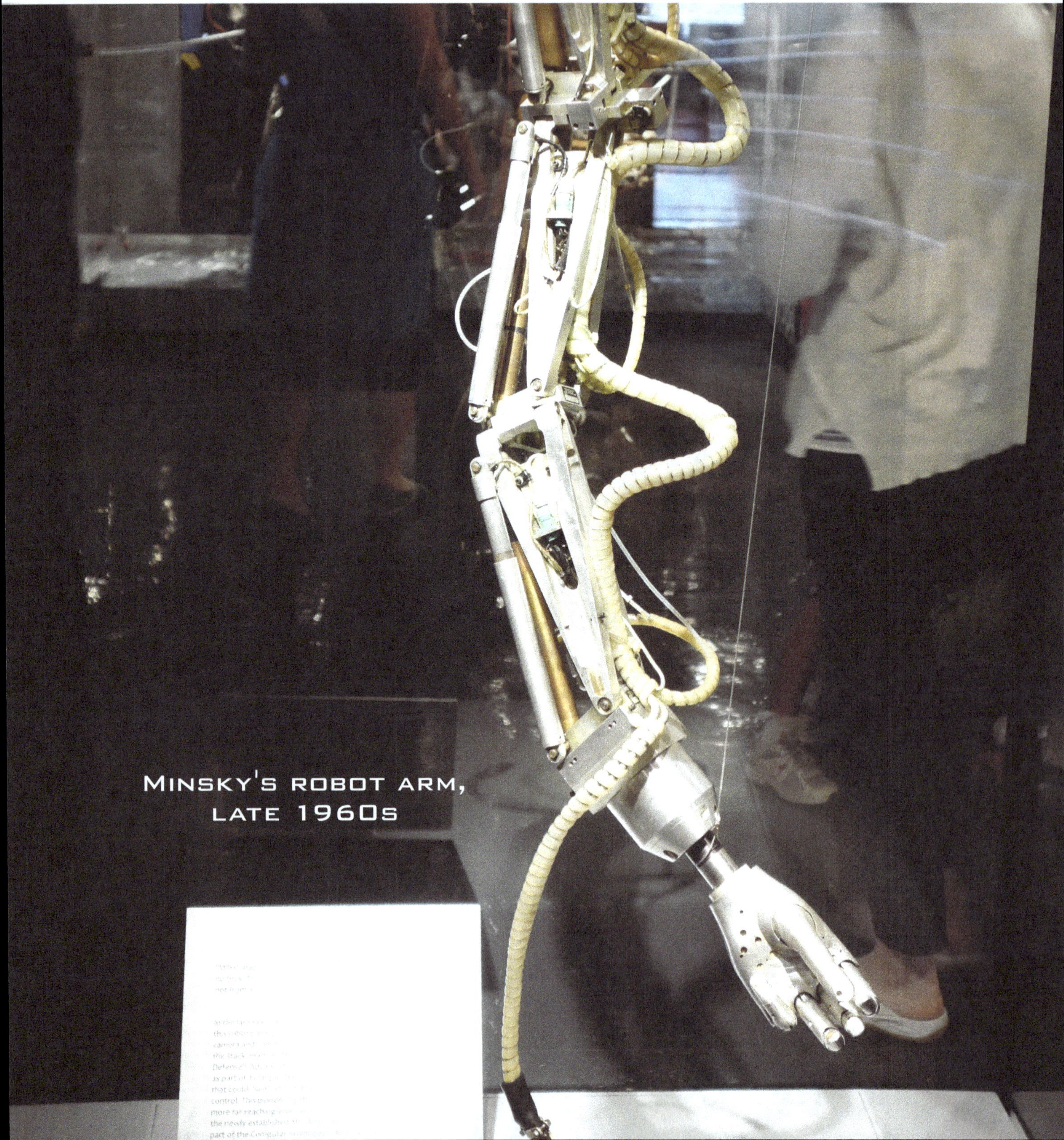

MINSKY'S ROBOT ARM,
LATE 1960s

1968

A Tentacle Arm with amazing movements like an octopus was designed by Marvin Lee Minsky, a pioneer in artificial intelligence. He founded the artificial intelligence lab at MIT.

1969

The Stanford Arm was designed by Victor Scheinman of Stanford University. It was a robotic arm that was powered by electricity and controlled by a computer.

1970

The Stanford Research Institute, SRI for short, developed the first robot that could move on its own. Known as Shakey, the robot was controlled by an early form of artificial intelligence.

1974

David Silver, a scientist from MIT, created the Silver Arm. It was a robotic arm that could do assembly of small parts and operated by touch through pressure sensors.

A TELEVISION CAMERA

1979

Hans Moravec built the Stanford Cart at Stanford University. It was able to navigate across a room filled with chairs without any human help. It had a television camera for its "eyes" so it could view the obstacles from multiple angles and choose a path. It could figure out the distance between itself and the chairs in the room.

1979 THROUGH TODAY

Since the Stanford Cart, robots have continued to evolve. They are being programmed with a higher level of intelligence than ever before. Robots are now being employed to do work in the military and in factories. They are at work on the International Space Station and some of them are vacuuming our floors!

BA
SYSTEMES
www.basystemes.com
MiR MiR100
INDUSTRIAL ROBOT

All the different capabilities of robots are steadily increasing. Roboticists are improving these systems to make robots even better in the future:

- Control systems to determine in what sequence the robot makes its moves

- Neural networks to help it "think" and move quickly

- Artificial intelligence to help it problem solve and process data

- Electronic circuitry to make it move and think smoothly from a central power source

- Sensors to help it observe and react to its environment

HOW ARE ROBOTS CLASSIFIED?

Robots can be classified into three basic types based on their circuitry.

Simple Level Robots These robots are machines that work automatically, but don't contain a complex circuit.

Middle Level Robots These robots can be programmed, but don't have the ability to be reprogrammed. They have circuits that are sensor-based and they can perform multiple tasks.

Complex Level Robots These robots have the functionality to be programmed as well as reprogrammed.

ROVER

USES OF ROBOTS

There are so many ways that robots are being used today. Here are some of the uses:

Outer Space

Robotic arms controlled by people are used in outer space to launch satellites or repair equipment.

FARMING

Some dairy farms are largely run by robotic processes today. Robots are also used to harvest and gather crops.

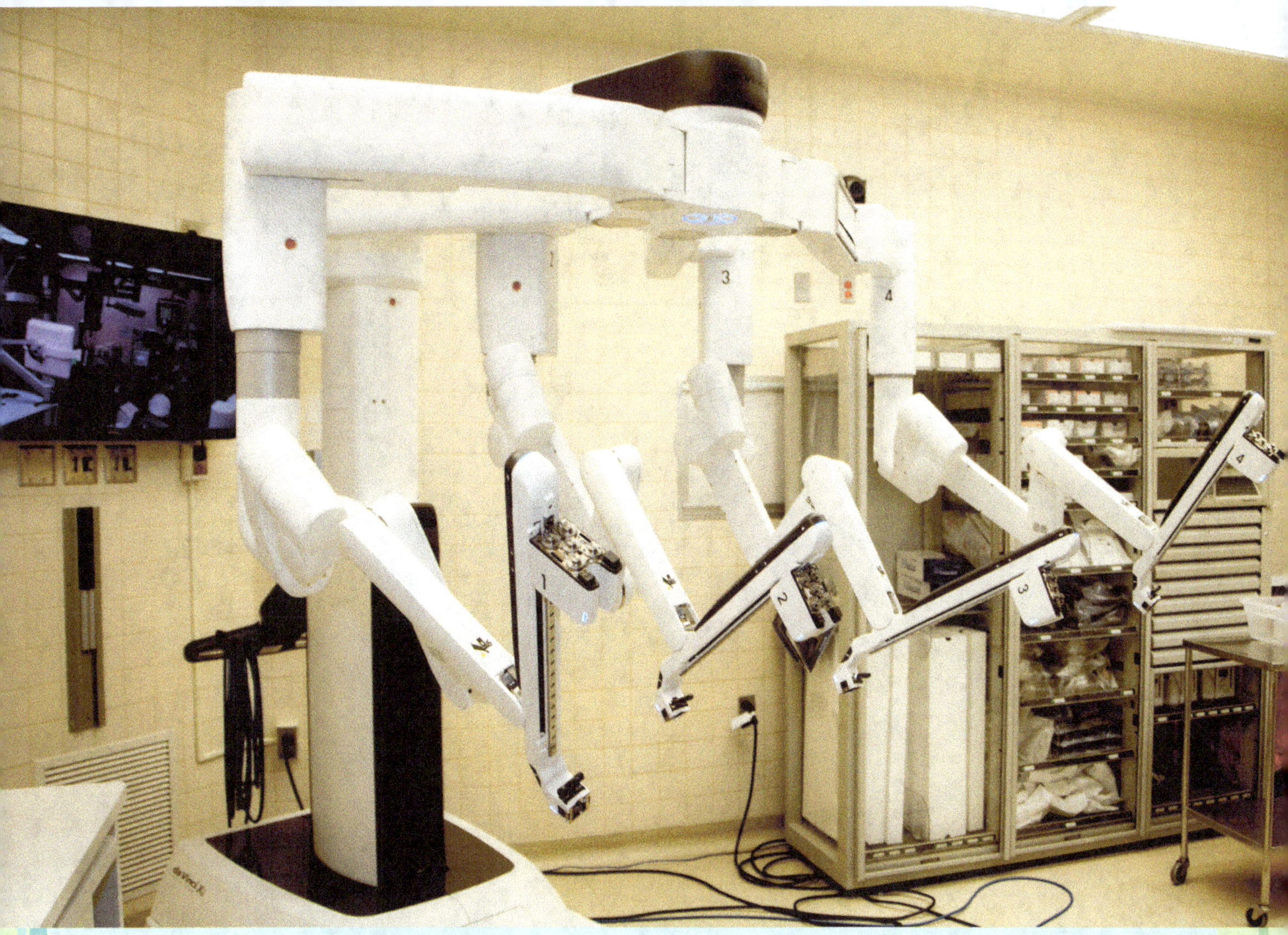

Hospitals

Robots are being developed that will help nurses to lift patients more easily without injury to themselves or the patients.

DIRT DEVIL BRAND
VACUUM CLEANER
POWER

The Artificially Intelligent Home

Robotic systems are part of some homes today. They manage security, air conditioning, and the consumption of energy. This helps the inhabitants of the home to control aspects of their home even if they are elderly and can't move easily themselves. Vacuum cleaners and mopping machines that are robotic can be purchased for home use.

Entertainment

Robotic toys and pets have been around for a while. Soon it may be possible to have a conversation with your robot.

Robots like the Mars rovers have been used to collect rocks and perform other experiments. The atmosphere at the surface of a volcano and life in the deepest trenches of the oceans have been studied by robots. They can enter dangerous environments in place of human beings.

Knightscope has created a sophisticated robot used for corporate security.

BIG DOG MILITARY
ROBOTS

Military Robots

Robot drones are used to gather intelligence. In the future, unmanned automobiles or other vehicles could be used to help clear minefields or to transport explosive materials.

The Car Industry

Robotic arms and other robotic devices have been used in car assembly work for decades. The food industry is starting to use them for tasks such as trimming and processing meats.

CAREERS IN ROBOTICS

If you're interested in the science of robots, you may want to train to become a roboticist. Science and mathematics are very important in this field. There's so much to know that even experts work in teams to design new robots.

ROBOTICIST

Puppy Robot
TEKNO

THE FUTURE OF ROBOTICS

As robots get more and more intelligent, they will be helping us with all sorts of tasks. It's also possible that they will be programmed to be more social and be our companions and friends.

SUMMARY

Robots have been popular in science fiction for decades, but today many types of robots are working alongside humans in factories, in the military, and out in space. Some of these robots are programmed to do simple manual tasks, but others are programmed to help with data processing or functions that require artificial intelligence. Robots don't "think on their own" without human programming or assistance yet, but they may in the future.

ANYBOTS
ANYBOTS
ANYBOTS

Awesome! Now that you know more about some of the different types of robots, you can read more about artificial intelligence and robots in the Baby Professor book **The Different AI Robots and Their Uses**.

Visit
BABY PROFESSOR
EDUCATION KIDS
www.BabyProfessorBooks.com
to download Free Baby Professor eBooks and view
our catalog of new and exciting Children's Books